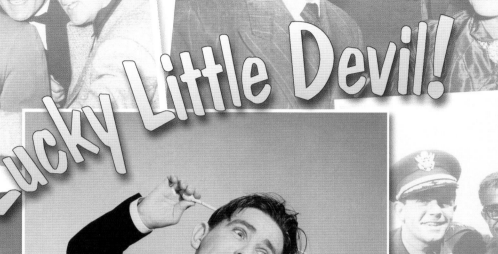

Lucky Little Devil!

Norman Wisdom

on the Island he's made his home

Written by

Norman Wisdom & Bill Dale

Edited by **Trevor Barrett**

Designed by **Tracey Harding**

Lily Publications
Limited

First published in 2003 by   **Lily Publications Ltd, PO Box 33, Ramsey, Isle of Man, IM99 4LP**

Telephone   **01624 898446**

Fax   **01624 898449**

ISBN   **1 899602 91 7**

Printed by   **Westdale Press Ltd, Cardiff**

Scanning   **Haven Colourprint Ltd/Lily Publications Ltd**

Acknowledgements   **Isle of Man Department of Tourism & Leisure, Clare Price, Timothy Cowsill, Keig's Ltd and John Watterson**

Publisher's Note   **Part of the proceeds of this title will be given to charities on the Isle of Man by Lily Publications Ltd**

CONTENTS

FUNNY HOW THINGS TURN OUT

MADCAP DAYS, HILARIOUS KNIGHT

I'D BE A FOOL TO LIVE ANYWHERE ELSE

FUNNY HOW THINGS TURN OUT

Norman Wisdom on the road to *Ballalaugh*

Now I don't want you thinking that just because I live in a lovely house on a beautiful holiday island, I sit around all day twiddling my thumbs. Tinkering with busy fingers on the piano keys and composing songs – now that's more like it!

Yes, I'm a lucky little devil all right. Things have turned out well for me, and I have a lot of kind people to thank for it. But I've never forgotten that life wasn't always as good as this.

I was born in Marylebone, London, and went to school in Scotland. I wasn't half tired when I got home every day!

In fact, I was born in sorry circumstances – my parents were very sorry!

Okay, I'm kidding – but as it happens these two old music hall gags carry more than a ring of truth.

I was born on 4th February 1915. I didn't have the happiest of childhoods and, to cut a long story short, I really *did* end up walking huge distances looking for work, food and a roof over my head.

I suppose I first learned the basics of acting at the age of 9, when I was hungry on the streets of London. My mother left my father because of his drinking and he pretty much left my brother Fred and I to fend for ourselves. We became street urchins. Standing outside the bakery window putting on a sad, sorry face sometimes worked a treat and we'd get a few scraps to eat.

Not that we enjoyed begging – but we had to be pretty imaginative to earn even a few pennies to buy food. We turned our hands to all sorts of jobs such as running errands, and when things got really bad we had to resort to stealing from barrows in the local market. In the early 1920s it was the only way to stay alive.

After being put into care – though not quite in the sense that unfortunate kids are these days because that sort of welfare just didn't exist then – things settled down to some extent and I found various part-time jobs. Delivery boy, hotel waiter, page boy in a ladies' club: all pretty humdrum stuff for a 14-year-old who yearned for something more interesting, exciting and different.

It was my Welsh workmate, Joe, who suggested we should try for mining jobs in Cardiff. I liked the idea and a few days later we left London and set off to walk the entire 183 miles. It took us two weeks and we slept rough in ditches and haystacks. Joe had promised me a bed in his parents' Cardiff home, but when we arrived in the Welsh capital he broke it to me that he hadn't even told them about me. Before I could take in what he was saying, he ran off down an alley and I never saw him again.

Alone and used, I ended up wandering around down by Cardiff docks, where tramp steamers took coal and anthracite from the South Wales valleys to all corners of the world. And I had a stroke of luck! A friendly security guard took pity and not only gave me food but also got me a job as a cabin boy. Suddenly I was boarding a cargo ship and, the very next day, setting sail for Argentina. In spite of Joe I was going to get the excitement I craved after all!

This is me in India shortly after I joined the Army. I'm in the unform of the **10th Royal Hussars** (the first of many royal connections in my life, though I wouldn't have believed that then!) in a place called Lucknow (there's that word 'luck' again!). I still have the spurs from my riding gear – hanging above my desk in the study at *Ballalaugh*.

More pictures from my far-off Army days. I loved sport and keeping myself in shape (all 8 stones of it!) and was pretty handy with my fists, becoming the undisputed **Flyweight Champion of the British Army in India** after winning the title and successfully defending it twice. And that's me on stage in a concert party, billed as Dizzie Wizzie. I look a bit more relaxed holding those two trees apart with a couple of my mates. That was at Naini Tal in the foothills of the Himalayas, where we were stationed temporarily.

Here I am singing **Don't Laugh At Me** — a song I wrote myself — in the 1953 film **Trouble In Store**. Luckily for me both were big hits and really set my career on the road.

A hug from my girlfriend? Cheeky monkey! His name was **Spike** and his behaviour was very unpredictable, but I wasn't told that at the time. Tragically, not long after this publicity shot was taken, he mauled his keeper to death. Didn't I tell you I'm a lucky little devil?

I know it's hard to believe – I look so young and dashing – but yes, this is me at home in 2003!

Five months later, after quite a few adventures and one or two harsh lessons in growing up, I was back in Wales and hunting for work again. I would have stayed with the ship for her next voyage but that was a non-starter because she was laid up and not going anywhere in a hurry.

So London beckoned once more – but only the prospect of living on the streets. I didn't know what to do. Until, as a chance remark, someone suggested joining the Army – and I did.

From that moment on I never looked back. I was soon on the high seas again, this time bound for India – much closer than Argentina! – and Army life proved to be absolutely brilliant. I had security, a roof over my head, clean clothes, regular meals, money in my pocket and, above all, lots of good mates. The happiest time in my life!

The Army also gave me my start in the entertainment business – although the opportunity came right out of the blue. Always keen to try anything new, I had joined the band and was soon learning to play all sorts of instruments. Boxing was another thing I was into. One day I was larking around, shadow boxing and pretending to be punched and knocked down – a routine which always had my mates in stitches – when the Entertainments Officer took me to one side and said, *"Wisdom, you're in the Concert Party."* You could have knocked me down with a feather!

I soon became the camp jester, billed on the handwritten posters as Dizzie Wizzie. I gained a reputation as a prankster because I just couldn't resist stunts such as tripping the other blokes up while marching on the parade ground, and marching with my right arm and right leg moving together, and holding the rifle upside down.

It may sound daft now, but despite all this the idea of becoming a professional comic had never entered my mind. Perhaps it never would if I hadn't been lucky enough to meet Rex Harrison at an Army charity concert after I'd served my term and left the service. He made a point of telling me I'd be mad not to pursue a professional career in showbusiness.

From such a talented man these were wonderful words of encouragement, driving me on throughout the tough early years as I auditioned here, there and everywhere to find work on the stage.

Vera Lynn was also exceptionally kind. When I was still an unknown, she big-heartedly gave up her prime spot for me at the Victoria Theatre in London in front of an audience which included many of the day's top agents and other very influential people.

And another to show great confidence in me in those early years was Lord Bernard Delfont, who later launched my film career.

I'll always remember the help and encouragement of these and other people who were either big names at the time or went on to become stars. Harry Secombe was one. When I was turned down at yet another audition, he said, *"Never mind, son – you'll make it."*

Luckily for me, good old Harry was right – and I've loved every minute of my entertainment career and wouldn't swap any of it.

Mind you, knowing what I know now, and given a second chance, I reckon I could do even better!

Above is my house on the Isle of Man. I designed it myself and was very keen to feature genuine Manx stonework throughout. I also supervised the construction and all the interior fixtures and fittings. When it came to choosing a name, what else could I call it but **Ballalaugh**? In Manx it means *'home of the laugh'*. So what do you think? I reckon even Mr Grimsdale would have to agree I've not done too badly for myself!

Retire? Me? No way – not while I'm having such a great time! In this recent scene from Roy Clarke's enduring **Last of the Summer Wine** – the world's longest-running TV sitcom – I'm playing the part of crackpot Billy Ingleton, who despite his advancing years still has serious aspirations for becoming a professional concert pianist. I was thrilled to get the part, and further appearances in this amazingly successful BBC series are planned. With me at the piano are fellow reprobate pensioners Norman Clegg (Peter Sallis), Compo (the late, great Bill Owen) and Foggy Dewhurst (Brian Wilde).

MADCAP DAYS, HILARIOUS KNIGHT

Bill Dale on the many faces of Britain's greatest clown

It's impossible to overstate the impact which Norman Wisdom has made on stage, television and the big screen throughout his long and remarkable career.

On the other hand, it could be argued that his success can be summed up in just a few short, simple words: fists, falls, faces, downs, ups and arise.

Fists? Well, after rejection by his father and such a tough childhood, it's not surprising he learned how to take care of himself. Before joining the Army and becoming featherweight boxing champion, he'd put his time as cabin boy on the voyage to Argentina to good use. Boxing sessions were a way for the crew to relax, and when Norman joined in he found he had a natural aptitude for it.

In Buenos Aires he even took on a local champ in a boxing booth and went the requisite three rounds, winning himself a fiver – which his shipmates promptly scarpered with and poured it down their necks in a bar.

Falls? Pratfalls were to become one of the keys to Norman's great showbusiness success, and in India, where he was a very able gymnast, he trained himself to fall off a galloping horse – forwards, backwards and sideways – without hurting himself as part of military displays.

Later in his career, he taught himself to skate after landing a lucrative role in a big ice spectacular on the strength that he already could! Within a few short weeks he'd become such a competent and confident skater that nobody doubted he'd been doing it for years, and daring falls and stunts became part of that act, and of subsequent even bigger and better ice shows too.

As for faces, nobody can act the fool as convincingly as Norman Wisdom has been doing for 60 years and more. In fits of hysterical laughter one moment and feigning tears of heart-touching sadness the next is a trick he perfected to mesmerising effect, and audiences have loved him for it.

His most famous song, **Don't Laugh At Me ('Cause I'm A Fool)**, could only have been written and performed by the man himself. It hit the number 1 spot in the charts and stayed in the top 10 for a record 9 months. And the 1953 film it came from, **Trouble In Store**, was a massive success too. Films which followed revealed many more faces of Norman, such as **The Square Peg** (1958) in which he played both Norman Pitkin and a German general.

Downs? Of course Norman's had his share – who hasn't? But a man who's survived such a painful childhood and then made an art out of riding the falls is better equipped than most to bounce back – and Norman always has, and without bitterness. Two failed marriages, a prolonged and much-publicised battle with the tax man, and being admitted to hospital suffering from malnutrition (because he was working so hard he wasn't feeding himself properly!) are episodes he would hardly consider high points.

But one memory which has haunted him more than most is that of the Christmas Day he spent all alone in a hostel at the age of 14, with nothing but his Christmas dinner for company.

Ups? Take your pick! For a man who is less than 5 feet tall, Norman Wisdom has scaled extraordinary heights – a comedy genius and a showbusiness giant.

His proudest moments, though, are undoubtedly the births of his children and grandchildren – as well as those precious seconds on Tuesday 6th June 2000 when he knelt before the Queen at Buckingham Palace.

From street urchin to knight of the realm.

Quite a rise, Sir Norman.

"Nice to see you, to see you, nice!" Two of Norman's biggest fans share an amusing few moments with him after a Royal Variety Performance. The one with the fancy headpiece is **Bruce Forsyth**.

"Let's start with the finger-pointing game and then we'll have a go at shaking each other's head off." **Freddie Starr** and Norman together on the Isle of Man in 2002 after Freddie arrived unexpectedly. *"I'm looking for somewhere cheap to stay,"* he said hopefully. *"Have you tried Blackpool?"* was Norman's quick reply.

"What a wonderful day for munching your way single-handed through a birthday cake and saying how's that for Wisdom teeth?"
Young upstart **Ken Dodd**, Britain's other great clown, can't remember which cubicle he stole the toilet brush from at Norman's 88th birthday bash in Liverpool. Gate-crashing soap stars are tickled pink.

Charlie Chaplin and other fans

Could Norman Wisdom have won the war simply by getting the enemy troops to roll on their backs in fits of laughter? He didn't get chance to find out.

Instead of taking orders on the battlefield, he was taking telephone calls in a basement bunker off the Edgware Road in London – one of Winston Churchill's top-secret wartime communications centres. Norman was one of a select team of people who manned the large switchboard and monitored and directed calls, speaking to people such as Eisenhower, Montgomery, General Patton and, of course, Churchill himself.

Despite Norman's attempts to rejoin the 10th Royal Hussars and see some real action, the job was classified as 'a restricted occupation' and exempted him from call-up.

Okay, so he didn't actually win the war – but in 1951 he **did** win over the men who had! At the El Alamein reunion in front of 6,000 men – including Monty, Ike and Churchill – Norman's performance went down a storm. "*That was one helluva show, young feller!*" Ike enthused, shaking Norman's hand.

It was also in the early 1950s that Norman's comic talents drew mighty praise from another world icon – the master himself, English-born Charlie Chaplin.

While in Hollywood with his agent, Norman cheekily called Chaplin's studios and asked to speak to the great man. To his amazement, Chaplin came to the 'phone and invited Norman over. In a meeting he'll never forget, Norman asked him, "*Could you do your walk for me?*" Chaplin replied, "*Only if you do your walk for me, Mr Wisdom,*" and went on to predict that "*One day, young man, you will be following in my footsteps.*"

Another comedian who Norman respected enormously was the great Sid Field. After Sid died in 1950, Norman received a telegram which read: "*If anyone can take his place we think it's you. Every success. Sid Field family.*"

What made the moment all the more poignant – and reduced him to tears – was the fact that the telegram was delivered to Norman as he prepared to go on stage, sat in the same dressing room in London's Prince of Wales Theatre which Sid had used for many years.

That telegram, preserved and framed, now takes pride of place in Norman's study in the Isle of Man. The message it conveyed was written more than 50 years ago – but today's comedians are just as appreciative of the Wisdom talent.

At Norman's 88th birthday bash in Liverpool, Ken Dodd paid him a very special tribute: "*He's a giant of a man, even though he could milk a cow standing up. He's our country's finest comedian, loved by everyone, young and old – a great and wonderful entertainer and a magical man. It's a shame there isn't more of Norman's kind of magic in this world today.*"

Then there are the words of Bruce Forsyth. "*We worked together many times,*" he recalls, "*and I'll never forget our two-man show for **Sunday Night at the London Palladium** in the 1960s. Norman is someone I will always, always admire.*"

And in summer 2002, Freddie Starr arrived unexpectedly on the Isle of Man – in search of a home! Now Freddie has often impersonated Norman, who has long been his idol, but this could be taking things *too* far!

"*I based my act on Norman because he's always been my hero,*" Freddie confesses. "*His energy, his enthusiasm and his genius inspired me to become a comedian. He's been the inspiration for many others too. He's up there alongside Chaplin and even now, in his eighties, he still has that something special – just look at how people's eyes light up when they see him.*"

Norman and Freddie are old pals, having worked together on stage. Freddie goes on: "*Norman's the number 1. I learned an enormous amount about timing, body language and facial expressions by*

" Look, Mo – if it's the only way to stop that bit at the back from sticking up – just do it!"
This heated moment with housekeeper Mo Faragher puts Norman in mind of his 1966 film **Press For Time**.

watching him over and over again, for hours on end, in his films and on stage. He is the ultimate professional. A gentleman, a true genius and a legend. I love him dearly."

And the admiration is mutual – because Norman reckons that of all the comics and entertainers over the years who have tried to imitate him, Freddie Starr is the best.

Another candidate who bears more than a passing resemblance to Norman is Lee Evans, who has the necessary qualifications of being small and very physical. He admits that Norman has been a major influence on his act and style of comedy.

Of course, you don't have to be a star to be a Norman Wisdom fan. Since he's been living on the Isle of Man, the person who's known him longer than anyone else is his housekeeper, Mo Faragher.

"Norman's great to work for but he can't half get you going sometimes!" says Mo, a star in her mischievous employer's eyes. *"He's always playing practical jokes and messing around, but it's just the way he is – everything is for fun in Norman's life and he's never been any different. If he was a child you'd probably smack him!"*

So much for the accolades – but has anyone ever been **wrong** about Norman Wisdom? Was anyone ever so far off beam that they wrote him off as a complete no-hoper, just as a BBC producer once famously did with The Rolling Stones?

In a word, yes. A line from his Army Education Course final report reads: *"The boy is every inch a fool but luckily for him he's not very tall."*

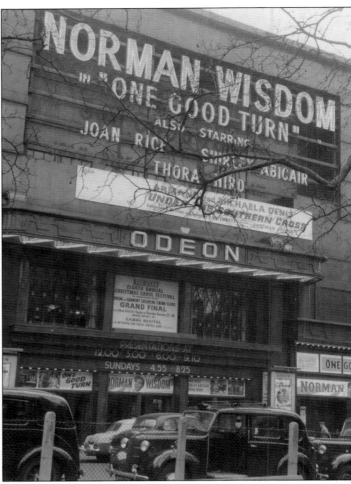

The Norman invasion of London! In the 1950s and 1960s you couldn't turn a corner in the West End without the name Norman Wisdom commanding your attention.

Snaps from the album and other snippets

Come on, be serious — who these days could possibly steal all the headlines and media attention from David Beckham?

Norman Wisdom!

This is precisely what happened in March 2001 in Albania, where Norman's films have made him a comedy legend. Loved by kids and adults alike, his presence with the England football team, who were in the capital Tirana for a European Championship qualifying match, was an occasion that caused no little media excitement.

It also added to Norman's vast and fascinating collection of photographs, which reveals a great deal about his megastar status over the years. In particular it focuses on the fact that during the 1950s and 1960s, at the peak of his big-screen career, he was the UK's leading cinema star, breaking box office records everywhere.

It's fair to say that since then only the James Bond phenomenon has had similar impact on audiences. The comparison holds up: **A Stitch In Time** (1963) knocked **From Russia With Love** off the number 1 spot. And, anxious not to get on the wrong side of 007 (and thereby proving that he's anything but a fool), Norman very sensibly became good friends with Sean Connery!

In this heyday period Norman made more successful films in a shorter space of time than probably any other star, with the possible exception of the silent movie era. Just as The Beatles had several hits in the charts at the same time, so the name and face of Norman Wisdom were appearing on cinema billboards all across the country, attracting audiences to a variety of hilarious and acclaimed screen comedies.

As well as Albania, where the people of an oppressive regime related to the little man (Norman Pitkin) standing up to authority, Norman's popularity spread across Europe, Australia, South Africa and the USA – and it remains strong today.

So does Norman's desire to keep working. He initially became a TV star when television was in its infancy, putting him ahead of virtually all other variety performers. Today it is still very much part of his life. As well as his continuing role in **Last of the Summer Wine**, he guested a spot in the BBC **Holiday** programme – showing off the Isle of Man, of course! – and an episode of **Casualty**, and receives a regular bombardment of scripts for a wide variety of assignments and cameo appearances.

And with all the enthusiasm and energy of a person only half his age, he also has a number of other major projects in the pipeline, notably his own movie – a long-standing ambition which he says is very close to his heart.

Entitled **Adam and Evil**, it is based on the J B Priestley story **Tober and the Tulpa** – a black comedy – and he's already cast Bo Derek to play the lead female part.

Who knows? With the Island's fledgling film industry really starting to roll, maybe Norman's movie will even be made on his beloved Isle of Man!

"Come on, Jimmy – just another two feet and you'll have swallowed the whole thing!" A publicity shot with comedian and TV star **Jimmy Edwards**.

One's favourite personages and other honours

Although he is naturally very proud of his OBE (which he was awarded in 1995) and his knighthood, Sir Norman Wisdom insists he's still just the same old Norman – a born entertainer who's happiest when he's making people laugh.

This simple modesty, so refreshing in a 21st-century culture of inflated celebrity egos, is one of the great qualities which endears the man to so many people.

Yet his lifetime achievements and honours add up to quite a list – and they show no signs of ending.

For example, his first of numerous appearances at Royal Variety Performance was as early as 1952, alongside other great comics of the day such as Tony Hancock, Terry Thomas, Jimmy Edwards, Arthur Askey, Vic Oliver and Ted Ray.

This Is Your Life has featured him twice, in 1957 and 1987.

In 1965 he won the Golden Flame Award (The Most Popular Artist of All Nations) at the Plata Film Festival in Argentina, and the following year his versatility rewarded him with the prestigious New York Critics Award for his performances in the Broadway stage musical **Walking Happy** – another milestone in his varied career.

Two years later he was asked by Richard Rodgers (as in Rodgers & Hammerstein) to play the title role in **Androcles & The Lion** – an American TV musical of George Bernard Shaw's play. Norman happily obliged, to great acclaim.

America offered him another golden opportunity with a leading role in the 1968 film **The Night They Raided Minsky's**. Norman seized it with both hands and was not only nominated for an Oscar but also attracted a favourable comparison with Buster Keaton from **Time** magazine.

Award has followed award throughout six decades of a breathtaking career. Further pinnacles of the incredible success story that is Norman Wisdom came in 1992, when he received the Lifetime Achievement Award at the British Comedy Awards, and in February 2002 in the shape of the Bernard Delfont Award for Outstanding Contribution to Showbusiness, presented at the Royal Variety Club Showbiz Awards.

So among Norman's millions of adoring fans around the world, is there one who stands out as a particular favourite of his?

Well here's a clue: she keeps corgis and lives in a nice little pad commonly referred to as Buck House.

As well as his Royal Command performances, Norman has met and amused the Queen on several occasions (and the Queen Mother *"I don't know how many times."*) In 1954 he entertained the royal family in the little theatre at Windsor Castle – a private show for the staff Christmas party – and it was revealed to him by a member of the household that the Queen can't keep a straight face when he's in the vicinity.

Maybe it was this bit of inside knowledge, never forgotten, which inspired him as he knelt before her in 2000 to receive his KB – Knight Bachelor for Services to Entertainment. As he retreated he couldn't resist bringing an air of fun to the proceedings by tripping over his own feet – an antic which the Queen reportedly found very amusing.

A framed photograph of the moment the honour was bestowed upon him stands on his piano. *"It was wonderful and I was very proud,"* says Norman. *"So were my son Nick and daughter Jacqui, my two guests for the day."*

By a remarkable coincidence, the occasion also saw two old rivals of the big screen cross swords again: Sean Connery was there too, receiving his knighthood.

One other point of royal interest is that although Norman lays no claim to blue blood (in fact he estimates he's currently about 50 millionth in line to the throne), he **can** boast that, like the Queen, his face has featured on postage stamps!

Arise, Sir Sean. Don't fall over, Sir Norman

By DALYA ALBERGE AND PAUL McCANN

Licensed to kneel: Sir Sean Connery, the former James Bond actor, who says that his knighthood is "an honour for Scotland"

Time for a laugh: Sir Norman Wisdom, the slapstick comedian, and Barbara Windsor, MBE, the former Carry On star

Certified! Documentary proof of Norman's knighthood and the fact that he has been granted the freedom of two cities – London and Tirana – and the Borough of Douglas. And who's that with him in the photograph he's holding? Can it really be **Stan Laurel** and **Oliver Hardy**?

A scene from **Man of the Moment** (1955) and behind the scenes during the making of **Press For Time** (1966) in which one of Norman's roles was to play his own grandfather, Wilfred.

Chernobyl's children and other good causes

There is another face to Norman Wisdom — a face I knew very little about until I first met him in 1993. The point of the meeting was to help a local Isle of Man charity to raise money for the construction of a hospice for the unfortunate children of Chernobyl, and I was immediately struck by Norman's amazing energy and willingness to do whatever he could.

This willingness saw him travel all the way to the Ukraine in the confines of a converted bus, so that he could see for himself the appalling conditions the people were having to endure because of the nuclear disaster. And, fittingly, the completed project resulted in the creation of The Norman Wisdom Children's Hospice.

Today he is President of Manx Mencap and still actively involved with charities across the Island. He attends numerous events, on occasions donning the famous suit and cap. And even his 88th birthday celebrations in Liverpool were used as the perfect excuse for fundraising.

Norman is also a great ambassador for the Isle of Man. There was no better example of this than the 2000-2001 BT Global Challenge Round the World Yacht Race, Norman's presence in Southampton for the official start attracting great interest and publicity for the Island's entry.

In recognition of his charity work and achievements in entertainment, a bronze statue of Norman, created by local sculptress Amanda Barton, sits outside the town hall in Douglas. The suit and cloth cap leave no room for doubt that the little figure sitting on the wooden bench represents one of the Island's most famous residents.

Norman as his own grandfather – an example of dual role playing – in **Press For Time** (1966).

Man of the Moment (1955) – in what looks suspiciously like a dress.

From the hilarious football match scene in **Up In The World** (1956).

"This is fantastic! I put six eggs in this basket this morning and look what they've hatched into!"
From the 1954 hit **One Good Turn**.

"Honest, sir – it wasn't me." Straight man **Jerry Desmonde** *(left)* worked with Norman over a 12-year period in 6 films (including this 1956 hit **Up In The World**) and many TV and stage appearances.

*"I keep telling you – I **haven't** knicked your lousy curtains. I got this cloak from Marks & Spencer in Douglas – and I'll show you the receipt to prove it."* Norman enjoyed all the female company in **Man of the Moment** (1955).

"Hello there. Has anyone seen that funny little fellow Norman Pitkin pass this way?"

George Formby, minus ukulele, proving that he wasn't always cleaning windows, and **Roy Castle** – a particular favourite of Norman's for his high-energy performances, great musical ability and the fact that he was also *"just a really nice bloke."*

Rhodesia (now Zimbabwe) Prime Minister Ian Smith gave Norman a copy of his book when they met in the late 1960s. At Norman's request he signed it 'Smudger Smith' (in the Army every Smith is a Smudger) and the book is one of Norman's treasured possessions in his *Ballalaugh* study.

"This suit ain't big enough for both of us."
Bought from a secondhand shop in Scarborough, the famous undersize suit appeared in the first Norman Pitkin film, **Trouble In Store**, in 1953 and over the years practically became a star in its own right! But there was no way it was ever going to survive Norman's hectic slapstick comedy antics, so several replacements had to be made during its long and distinguished career – and Norman's, of course!

Following pages
Where there's **Hope**, there's Wisdom!

"When I agreed to fly over from the States and share the bill, Norman, I didn't mean the one in the restaurant."
Liberace was popular with British TV viewers and is seen here after they both starred at the London Palladium.

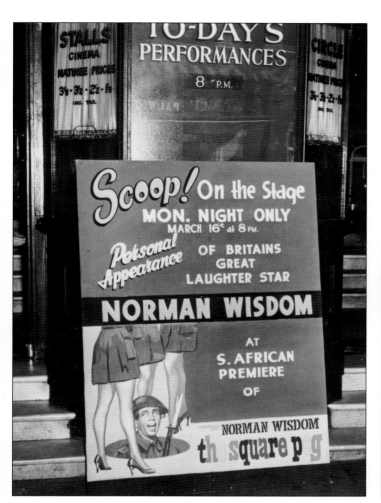

Norman has been in demand everywhere! The poster *(top left)* announces his personal appearance for the South African premiere of **The Square Peg**, and the press shots show him with co-star **Sally Smith** at the Theatre Royal in Nottingham (the message on the board has nothing to do with their personal lives!) applying a gentle back massage to one of the dancers.

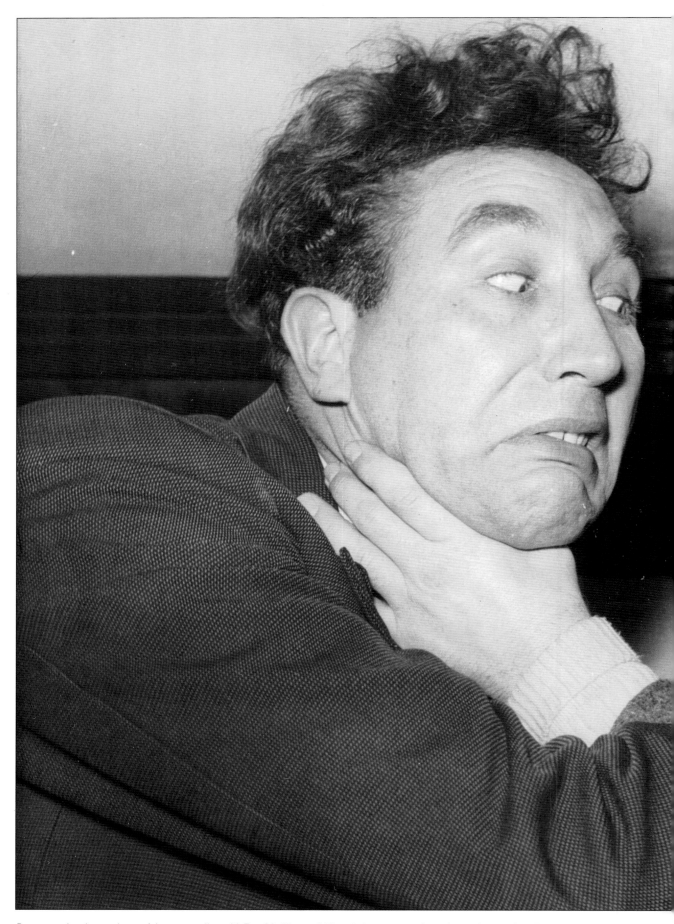

Demonstrating the gentle art of throat wrestling with **Frankie Howerd**. Though they never performed a routine together, they were often on the same bill on stage and TV.

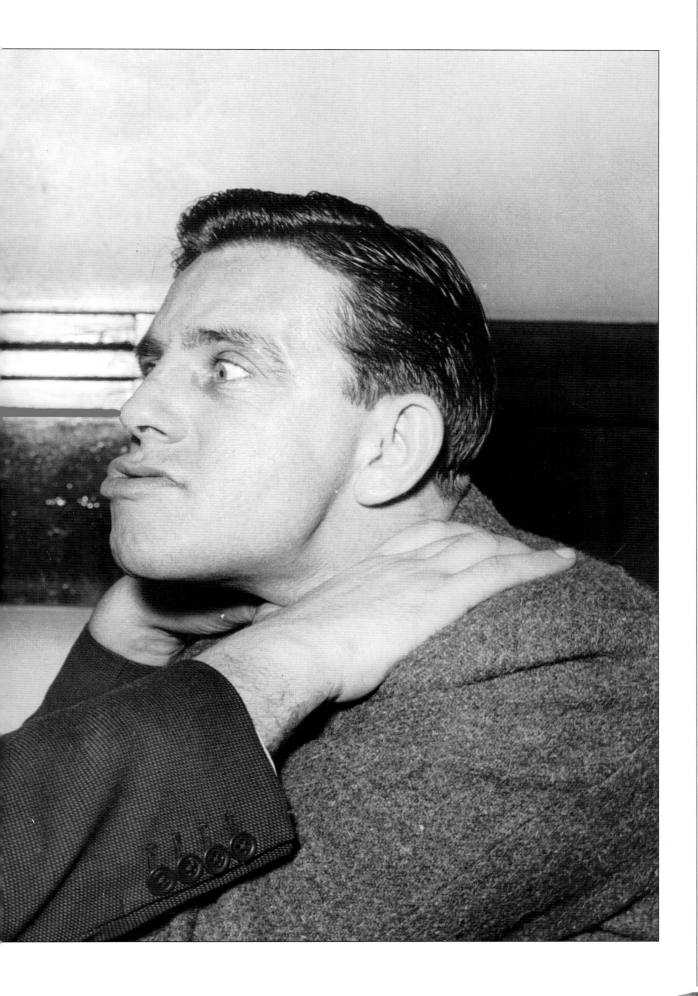

"Never mind these two – just focus on the pretty one!" In London with **Ella Fitzgerald** and **Harry Secombe**.

Hayley Mills and her famous parents in the 1960s.

Another Royal Variety Performance moment – this time with **Claire Bloom** and **Lord Snowdon** – while comedy actress **Carol Channing** tells Norman the one about the Englishman, the Irishman and the Scotsman.

Opposite page
And one of those Sammy moments: dressed for Uncle Sam's Army and in the company of the incredible **Sammy Davis Junior**, during a break in filming.

Edward G Robinson is more interested in the camera than whatever it is that's distracting Norman and film producer **Stan Houston**.

"I've always fancied this pair."
Sally Norman *(left)* and **Dylis Watling** – stage co-stars.

Lucky little devil! In the company of Hollywood legend **Joan Crawford** and the lovely **Jill Dixon** (in the 1957 film **Just My Luck**, which also starred Margaret Rutherford).

The Daily Telegraph

ce will not need Nato, says French military chic

wn yields
accine
cattle

The Norman conquest of Albania

Ka vetem një Pitkin! (There's only one Norman Wisdom!)

In the media spotlight: Norman's enormous popularity in **Albania** is all down to his films, which have always portrayed him as the little man and underdog battling against impossible odds and power-hungry bosses. And, as Norman points out, *"In my films there is no sex, no bad language, no car crashes and no crime."*

And in 2002, Norman returned to the country again with comedian **Tony Hawks** and songwriter **Tim Rice** to produce a record for the Albanian market. **Big In Albania**, written by Tony and Tim, immediately went into the charts and at the tender age of 87 Norman became the oldest singer to reach the top 20 in any chart anywhere in the world.

THE  TIMES

35p

WEDNESDAY MARCH 28 2001

ZW   www.thetimes.co.uk

y: what you should e achieved by 30

TIMES ②

Why Judaism is dying

Jonathan Sacks interview

TIMES ②

lines buy ntrol of r traffic

"This is your captain speaking: we should be landing as soon as the accountant gives us the all clear"

duce delays and rejected the claims of some opponents that the privatisation would create a "Railtrack of the skies".

The group will pay the Government around £800 million for 46 per cent of NATS and, in return, promise to invest £1 billion over the next seven years in new systems and a new centre at Prestwick. The 5,500 employees will each be given shares worth just under £1,000. The Government will retain a 49 per cent stake and appoint several directors to the board.

A big expansion in the capacity of the system is being prepared by the seven airlines, which own equal shares in the consortium. They are expected to announce details of how the growth will be achieved closer to the completion date of June 1.

Air travel is growing by 5 per cent a year in this country and total passenger numbers are expected to double by 2015, but the European Civil Aviation Conference issued a warning last week that European airspace faces gridlock by 2005 unless action is taken to boost capacity.

While the Airline Group, whose other members are Britannia, Monarch, easyJet and Airtours, pledged that the safety of passengers in British airspace would be its main objective, it hinted at expansion plans abroad.

Britain is the first country in Europe to experiment with privatisation of air traffic control services and others, such as The Netherlands, will be watching closely. NATS is now well-placed to bid if they decide to follow suit.

The group also claimed that the Public-Private Partnership would "act as a catalyst for the development of a single European sky". Under the proposal, which is fiercely opposed by the Conservatives, all European airspace would be centrally controlled, allowing extra flights to be squeezed in and delays reduced.

The controllers' main union, the IPMS, was pleased that the only not-for-commercial-return bid had won. It had said that the pursuit of profit could lead to short cuts, possibly leading to an air disaster. "But we do not welcome the Public-Private Partnership. It is a major distraction at a time of momentous change," the general secretary, Paul Noon, said.

The hero and the newcomer: Sir Norman Wisdom with the relatively unknown David Beckham in Albania

So who is that man with Norman Wisdom?

By Matt Dickinson in Tirana **and Joanna Bale**

DAVID BECKHAM may have one of the most famous faces in football, but as he trained for tonight's World Cup qualifier in Albania he was upstaged by an octogenarian with a cheeky grin.

Sir Norman Wisdom is idolised by Albanians, who remembers him for brightening their lives with slapstick during 40 years of communism.

The 86-year-old comedian is visiting Albania to open a hospital, but he will also watch tonight's match — which he predicts England will win 12-0 — and yesterday he dropped by to watch the team practice. He was mobbed by 400 autograph hunters; Beckham faced a gaggle of three teenage girls.

In the years of Enver Hoxha's regime, Albanian families devoured endless repeats of Wisdom's films as a relief from dreary state television. They were allowed because they appeared to contain a Marxist message, with Wisdom's Norman Pitkin character the plucky proletarian, refusing to be crushed by his social superiors.

To the people, he became the great "Pitkin", but the comedian has another take on his success: "They couldn't show sex or car crashes or bad language but apparently they loved my films. They were good films, weren't they?"

During the precarious post-communist years, his popularity has remained undiminished.

Leading article, page 19
Match preview, page 36
The wild frontier, Times 2

*"So who **is** that man with Norman Wisdom?"* asked the front page of **The Times** on Wednesday 28th March 2001. And the photograph of Norman meeting children from **Chernobyl** at a charity appearance on the Isle of Man provides further proof that it's not just the David Beckhams of this world who are the idols of young people.

So who's the best one in this picture? *"I am,"* says **George** confidently, flanked by members of **The Bachelors**. And is that a spare head stuck to Norman's shoulder as he watches the action ringside? No – it's boxer **Freddie Mills** trying to get a better view from the cheap seats as he muscles in between Norman and **Stewart Grainger**.

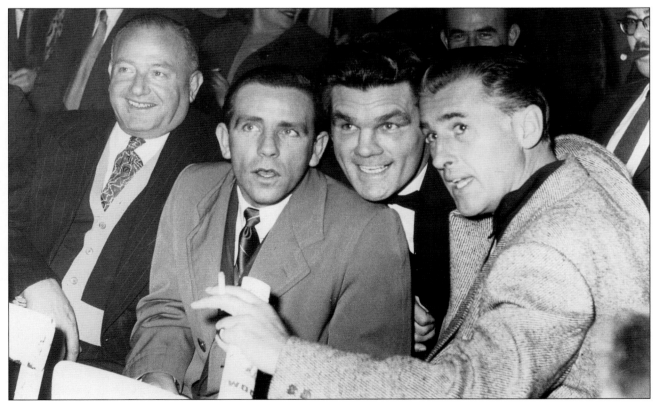

Opposite page
In the 1959 film **Follow A Star**, Norman Pitkin handed over the baton to frenzied conductor **Norman Truscott**.

Norman at work on the Isle of Man – for the BBC's popular **Holiday** series. The photographs show him at Laxey, generously signing autographs for fans. By sheer coincidence, the producer and director for the shoot was Norman's nephew **Peter Wisdom**.

*"Honest — it was **this** big — never seen a kipper like it!"*
Norman playing ambassador for the Isle of Man at the start of the **BT Global Challenge Round the World Race** of 2000-2001 in Southampton, with the Mayoress of Douglas Councillor **Doreen Kinrade**.

And below, there she blows! The Island's entry, **Isle of Man**, off Wellington, New Zealand.

As **President** of **Manx Mencap**, Norman is used to raising big cheques for good causes.

Piece of cake! **Norman's 80th birthday party** was probably the biggest ever, with 7,000 Isle of Man children and the media packed into Summerland, Douglas – an event which kick-started the fundraising appeal for the children of Chernobyl and led to the creation of the Norman Wisdom Children's Hospice in the Ukraine.

Another charity close to Norman's heart is the **Roy Castle Lung Cancer Foundation**.

Withdrawal symptoms: Norman Pitkin got a little carried away for this building society publicity campaign shown across the UK.

Former England, Liverpool, Chelsea and Aston Villa striker **Tony Hateley** is a close friend of Norman's and his 'minder' at charity golf days.

"Exactly the pyjamas I'm looking for!" At a charity event in the mayor's parlour at Southampton town hall.

Snap happy: photographer **Andrew Barton** putting Norman in the frame for a series of **Age Concern** Christmas cards, which completely sold out.

"*Cor blimey! Don't he look daft in that cap?*" With **Councillor George Chatel** when he was Mayor of Douglas.

"*Happy birthday to you..*" sings **Marilyn** as Norman tries to hold his excitement.

Not content with being made a **Freeman of the Borough of Douglas**, Norman insisted on bringing his bronze double with him. Pictured with past **Douglas Mayoress Raina Chatel** and **Mayoress June Craine**, Norman is seated by the famous statue, now a permanent feature outside Douglas town hall.

Norman receives the Freedom of Douglas.

"Ooh – you little tinker!" "And so are you," replies the **Queen Mother**. The meeting with **Princess Alexandra** was slightly more formal.

Tynwald Day – the Isle of Man's National Day, celebrated every July – was graced by the presence of **the Queen** and the **Duke of Edinburgh** in 2003.

Above
Maxine Cannon of the Isle of Man Post presents a special stamps portfolio to Her Majesty, with novelist **Barbara Taylor Bradford** and Norman looking on.

"Are you absolutely sure you wouldn't like me to autograph your handkerchief, sir?"

A much earlier meeting with the Queen, including the great **Bob Hope**.

"Most kind, Sir Norman. One has always wanted one's own set of dominoes." **The Queen** looks delighted with Norman's gift – a selection of delicious Manx cheeses.

"The name's Wisdom. Just make it out for a million ." Radio and press interviews are all part of a busy knight's work.

Norman insisted on staying at the Queen's side and paying her close attention, much to her amusement.

I'D BE A FOOL TO LIVE ANYWHERE ELSE

Norman Wisdom on the Isle of Man

So what's the big attraction of the Isle of Man?

Well, I can certainly tell you what is for me — and why I'm very happy to stay here. It's been an adventure since 1978, when I was lucky enough to do a 3-month summer season at the Gaiety Theatre in Douglas.

That summer was the first time I'd ever been to the Isle of Man, and it came as a big surprise. As far as I remember I didn't have any preconceived notions, but even so the stunning scenery and the sheer beauty of the coastline took my breath away and really opened my eyes.

"At last — you're here. I've been stood here for ages waiting for you to reach this page."

Over those weeks and months I soon started to appreciate other things that make this place so special. The Manx people, for one — so warm and friendly and welcoming. It was easy to understand why the crime rate was so low, and still is — even today you can go anywhere feeling completely safe and secure.

It took me a little while longer to understand that it's probably the Island's self-governing independence which gives it a very different feel from mainland Britain. The attitude is more relaxed, easy going, carefree, unhurried — and it's very contagious. In fact the Manx have a saying — *'Traa dy-liooar'* ('time enough') — which just about sums up the pace of life here.

Of course, there are lots of other reasons why people come to the Isle of Man. The amazing vintage railways, the TT and other racing, fantastic fishing, lovely seaside resorts, some of the best walking country you'll find anywhere, and all this wonderful clean fresh air. And did I mention the golf? Would you believe that on an island this size there are 9 terrific golf courses? It's true!

Anyway, having decided that the Isle of Man was definitely for me, I made the move across the Irish Sea in 1980 and spent a lot of time driving around to find the perfect spot. My first choice was a picturesque site in the valley at East Baldwin, not far from Douglas, set amongst trees and close to the river.

But during the time that the house was being built I realised that the north and west coasts tend to benefit from the best weather. The upshot was that I never moved into that house. As lovely as its location was, for me it just couldn't compete with the idyllic spot I eventually opted for — the place where a small run-down old cottage stood in a wonderful position in remote Kirk Andreas, in the north, with glorious views across the countryside to the mountains beyond.

At first the owner of the cottage wasn't interested in selling it — but then wrote to me out of the blue in the hope that I hadn't changed my mind. I couldn't believe my luck. The deal was dealt, the tumbledown cottage tumbled down (with a little help from a demolition team) and in its place I designed and built *Ballalaugh*, my dream home, from scratch. It was completed in 1984 and I've lived here ever since.

The garden at *Ballalaugh* is such a delightful place to practise – and every day I'm getting ever more proficient in the ancient art of bench sitting.

"..and then we'll tell everybody Bill Dale's won the lottery and suggest they should send him begging letters!" Discussing the day's most urgent priorities with personal assistant and secretary **Sylvia Evans.**

"Too late, Rodney. They've spotted us." **Rodney Done** is not only Norman's gardener of many years – they are also very good friends, and Norman is quick to point out that the beautiful garden is all down to Rodney's green fingers.

"Give me good old traditional British grub any day of the week. Such as a nice strong curry!" Norman loves his cottage pie, roast beef, bangers and mash – and cod'n'chips of course – and sits down to Sunday dinner at one o'clock, dead on the dot, as he's always done. His more Eastern palate was acquired in his Army days in India.

"I love coming to this supermarket. The kiddies' rides are almost real." These days Norman's scooter tends to stay in the garage, but he's a regular visitor to Manx TT Races.

"Look at this for progress! Here I am demonstrating the altogether more advanced discipline of bench lying."

"Owzat!" Former England wicketkeeper **Jack Russell**, a lifetime fan of Norman's, is now perfecting his strokes with an artist's brush and he popped into *Ballalaugh* for a spot of painting. The respect is mutual. Norman, a member of Lords Taverners, is mad about the game and his son Nick has played for Sussex.

"Don't be a fool, Roy – you've got much more chance of hitting it with the blunt end. It's bigger."
Norman regularly challenges good friend **Roy Dowie** to snooker or table tennis at Roy's house in St John's.
"I have to keep my eyes peeled," says Roy. "It's amazing how many times I suddenly find a red ball sitting right over the pocket when it's Norman's turn."

"Don't worry, Colin. Just smile and everybody will assume you know how to play it." **David Yuen** and **Colin Norman**, friend and personal music director who's worked with Norman for more than 40 years, are guaranteed a grand time whenever they visit.

Time's flown by and it's hard to believe that I've now been resident on the Isle of Man for 23 years – more than a quarter of my whole life! And yet I still get a kick out of jumping into the car every day and exploring the narrow tracks, lovely lanes and country roads that criss-cross the Island. There are nearly 700 miles of roads – so I've plenty of opportunity to get completely lost, and sometimes do!

One of the things I really love about the place is that there's plenty of space. Douglas is a busy capital but aside from that you're not exactly falling over people all the time. Large chunks of land are uninhabited and unless the Vikings invade again nothing's ever likely to change that.

It's 33 miles from one end of the Island to the other, and it's about 13 miles wide. This works out that you're never more than about 5 miles or so from the sea.

And another thing I love: although the Manx have their own ways of doing things, and their own Gaelic language (which admittedly hasn't been in everyday use for a very long time now), driving is on the left and all the other hallmarks of a sensible civilisation also apply! So it's home from home, with all the extra benefits of being permanently on holiday.

Do I have a typical day or daily routine?

Well, my engagements diary still keeps me pretty busy – particularly charity dos – and my mind's always full of new music and song ideas. I've written about 30 songs and was co-screenwriter on several of my films, and throughout my career all my comedy material has always been original. I do my composing on a French Erard grand piano in the lounge, my favourite room. The house has quite a few European influences about it – a strong Spanish feel and lots of Spanish and Italian furniture.

Looking towards **Peel** from Jurby in the north-west.

I suppose the same applies to the car – a BMW. I've always liked a nice motor, and even on the Island's narrow and twisting roads a biggish car like this is easy and fun to drive, and of course very comfortable.

If you were to ask me my favourite Isle of Man places, I'd rattle off a whole string of names as long as your arm. And getting back to the question of a daily routine, I have to confess that although I'm a long-standing resident (okay, short-standing in my case!) I behave more like a tourist. Even in the depths of winter, the weather has to be pretty awful to stop me from taking my daily fix of driving!

I don't walk as much as I used to, but for those who love walking I don't know of a better place to do it than the Isle of Man. The landscape and the opportunities and the variety are just fantastic.

Let's imagine for a moment that you've turned up early at *Ballalaugh* one morning and asked me to give you a bit of a conducted round-the-coast tour — by car, of course!

Okay — hop in, and seat belt on! Our first stop has to be the local post office in Andreas for my newspaper. This *is* a daily ritual, and Julie Claydon who runs it has got to know me pretty well by now. To tell you the truth I think she's always wanted to recruit me as a paper boy but is too polite to ask if I'm old enough!

Taking in the sweep of the north-west coast from **Devil's Elbow.**

Daily male — and the other one is **Julie Claydon**.

Ballaugh old church, in the north of the Island.

Here's a pointer to a bit of the Manx language. **Raad Ny Foillan** means *'Road of the Gull'* – the 90-mile coastal footpath that enables you to walk around the Island's entire coastline, if you have the energy! This is the longest of the long-distance paths, and there are lots of much easier routes and trails to follow. It's a breathtaking way to see the Isle of Man – and it keeps you fit!

Normally I'd take a scenic route back to *Ballalaugh* to read my paper, turning off into the first lane that catches my eye and tootling through the lovely countryside and quiet roads which are so typical of the Island's northern plain – a brilliant area for getting on your bike, by the way, because it's pretty flat here compared with most other parts. Today, though, as you're my special guest passenger, let's head to the west coast and drive down to Peel.

Now this is what you call a coast road. Even though it's in an elevated position, well above sea level, it really does follow the twists and turns of the shoreline for long stretches and the views are just fabulous. On a clear day you can see the Mountains of Mourne beckoning across the Irish Sea, about 60 miles or so away.

Taking it at a leisurely pace – if you rush it you miss the scenery – it's about a 30-minute drive from my house to Peel. This old fishing port used to have a big thriving fleet of herring boats, and although over the decades the fishing industry has declined here as elsewhere, Peel is still famous for one of the Island's most popular exports – Manx kippers!

In summer the place on the quayside where the kippers are smoked is open to visitors and you can see them doing it in the time-honoured fashion. And you can buy some, of course – even send kippers by post to a friend or relative!

As for me, I prefer another Peel delicacy – ice cream. I have a bit of a passion for it, and enjoy it best when I drive out to the breakwater and take in the view while I'm tucking in. I'm telling you, this ice cream takes some licking!

If I'm there late in the day I'll catch another treat which Peel often serves up – a truly spectacular sunset, made all the more dramatic as the fading light draws a stark silhouette of the ruins of Peel Castle against the darkening skyline.

So where do we go from here? Let's carry on along the west coast road through Glen Maye, about 3 miles south of Peel. Here we'll find some of the oldest woodland on the Island, as well as a gorge and waterfall which are as pretty as a picture.

There are 17 glens on the Isle of Man, sensitively managed to preserve their natural state. If you want some real peace and quiet, or you're looking for a bit of creative inspiration, a glen is one of the best places to head for.

A little further down the coast road is one of my favourite beauty spots – Niarbyl. We'll have to take a slight detour down a narrow road to get to it, but it's worth it. The truth is that there's very little here – but that's exactly what makes it so special.

Niarbyl is completely unspoiled and you can sit in the car or on the rocks and take in the views across the bay and just wonder at the wild beauty that spreads out before you as far as the eye can see. Actually, there *is* something of interest here – an old fisherman's cottage which featured in that very funny hit comedy film *Waking Ned*. The story was set in Ireland but the film was shot on the Isle of Man – and when you come to Niarbyl you can understand why.

Ireland's **Mountains of Mourne** fade away into the sunset.

"I'm not sure about this one either, Diane – we'll have to try another dozen or so."
Diane Christian is no sucker when it comes to Norman's antics in the Peel ice cream parlour.

*"Okay, I admit it – I **am** Freddie Starr. **Now** will you put me down?"*
Young fans take a hands-on approach in the hope that some of that sparkling talent will rub off.

"Sorry, lads – you're wasting your time – you can't play darts with me. My head went blunt years ago." A motorcycle presentation in **Peel**.

The factory in **Peel** where Manx kippers are smoked over oak chips.

Peel harbour

We won't bother taking another detour, but for me the area inland here is just as interesting as the coast. The countryside is amazing and varies so much. One minute there's a coastal view across open fields, the next it's a green valley where you can't see the wood for the trees, or a glen with waterfalls and streams. And exploring the farm lanes and narrow tracks is my cup of tea – I can't wait to see what's round the next corner. Okay, sometimes it's a tractor or a flock of sheep and I'm stuck, but that's all part of the fun!

Now we're close to Douglas, the capital of the Isle of Man. It's a really bustling town, with some terrific shops. For my knighthood ceremony at Buckingham Palace in 2000 I hired my morning suit from Peter Luis, where I'm a regular customer. Another shop I frequent here is Marks & Spencer. I just love their curries (a throwback to my Army days in India!).

The place in Douglas I really want to show you though is a road called Marine Drive. It lies on the clifftop above the harbour at Douglas Head. The road used to run to nearby Port Soderick, but quite a few years back a landslide sent a section of it avalanching into the sea and these days you can only drive so far. But it's a great place to park and walk and take in the terrific views. Looking out over Douglas Bay, for example, you can see the ferries coming in from Heysham, Liverpool and Ireland, and the planes are really low as they prepare to touch down at Ronaldsway.

At this point we've already driven about three-quarters of the way around the Island's coast roads! To complete the circuit and return to *Ballalaugh* in the north, we have 2 options: up over Snaefell mountain (at 2,036 feet/621 metres the highest point on the Island) or stick to the coast road by driving along Douglas's sweeping 2-mile promenade and heading towards Laxey, with the tracks and pantographs of the Manx Electric Railway running alongside the road as we climb up to Onchan Head.

Whenever I choose the latter route I take the narrow turn-off to Laxey old village. Laxey is a very picturesque and interesting place. For one thing it has the huge waterwheel, a legacy of the old mining industry, and for another the railway station is the only junction in Britain with lines of two different gauges – one gauge for the Manx Electric Railway and one for the Snaefell Mountain Railway, which takes you to the summit. Laxey old village is also very charming.

If we decide on the alternative route – the mountain road, passing the peak of Snaefell – we'll have spectacular views as we descend through Sulby Glen. The Sulby is the longest river on the Isle of Man – less than 11 miles mind – and it joins the sea at Ramsey, which is the second largest town on the Isle of Man and once an important centre for shipbuilding. I shop here sometimes, as it makes a nice change from Douglas and of course is much closer to home.

We're close to *Ballalaugh* now, and I often drive past the house I used to rent when I first came to the Island – the Coach House in Bride. Now and again I'll also head for the lighthouse at the Point of Ayre.

"Come here, you little beauty!" That's **Peel Castle** in the background.

This is as far north as you can go if you want to stay on dry land – which I tend to prefer when I'm driving! – and on the way here there are some pretty thatched cottages. Call me nosy, but if I see a nice place for sale and it looks like there's no one about I'll sometimes have a quick shufty round. Not that I'm planning to buy – it's just that I love seeing the home improvements other people have made!

The area of coastline on which the lighthouse stands is called the Ayres. It's only a few miles from where I live and a very awe-inspiring and wild environment. People come here for long walks and the isolation and to enjoy the seabirds and 18 miles of sandy beach which ribbons the north-west coast. Anglers like this place too but need to have their wits about them to battle with the fast-flowing tides that rip by viciously with no regard for anything in their path. If ever you need reminding of the raw power of nature, the Ayres is the place to come.

It's only a short drive back to *Ballalaugh* and the end of our lightning coastal tour. There's much much more to see, of course – and I'll leave the photographs to show you at least some of it. After all, a picture tells a thousand words.

It's been a pleasure to give you a few glimpses of my home and life here on the Isle of Man. And I hope that some day soon we'll meet again – if not in person on the Island then at least in the pages of another book!

More Peel appeal: the harbour in late evening, and sunset over the castle and **St Patrick's Isle**.

"Somewhere, under the rainbow..." is **Patrick**.

Niarbyl Bay, shrouded in mist.

A couple of thatched fishermen's cottages near the shore in a remote, wild and completely unspoilt bay – this is the beauty of **Niarbyl**. No wonder it's a favourite location for movie makers! Scenes from the hit comedy **Waking Ned** were filmed here.

The sheltered haven of **Fleshwick Bay**, near Port Erin.

The old mine workings in **Rushen** – the parish that gives its name to Castletown's castle.

Sunset over **Bradda Head**, Port Erin, in the south-west, as seen from the Langness peninsula in the south-east.

"I could stand here all day watching other people work. There's something about **Port Erin** that quietly screams at you to take it easy and behave as if you're on holiday – so I usually do! And why are boats so fascinating to look at even when they're beached and not going anywhere? I think I'd better sit down. I've worn myself out now saying all that!"

Houses and gardens on **Port Erin's** lower promenade.

Here we are on the most westerly point of the Island, right in the south-west corner. Across the **Sound** there is the **Calf of Man**. It's a bird sanctuary. In fact, this whole area is important for wildlife and seabirds. It's a pretty wild sort of place.

This is a view from a high point known as the **Sloc**. The boats in the harbour are at **Port St Mary**.

Preparing to do its work as the sun sinks into the sea – the lighthouse at **Langness**. And below, how it looks viewed from the hills.

Opposite
Derby Fort on **St Michael's Island** at Langness.

Looking down from **Marine Drive** – the dramatic Douglas-Port Soderick through road (until a landslide bisected it).

Here you can see just how spectacularly **Marine Drive** edges it way above the rocky shoreline.

Doesn't it put you in mind of Edith Nesbit's wonderful story, **The Railway Children**? The amazing thing about it is that this isn't a line run by the volunteers of a steam preservation society – it's part and parcel of the Island's everyday transport system. The biggest reinvestment since the **Isle of Man Steam Railway** opened in the 1870s has seen most of the 15-mile track completely renewed.

Farming is an important industry on the Isle of Man, and sheepdog trials are as much a tradition here as elsewhere in the British Isles. So are the Island's agricultural shows. They're very colourful and draw big crowds.

This is me in the 1980s when I was guest of honour for the Isle of Man Cycle Week. Trying to stop me from nicking the motorbike is **Steve Joughin** – the Island's most successful professional cyclist.

And here I am with the 1993 international winner – Scotsman **Brian Smith**.

These are the **Douglas horse trams** which run up and down the promenade in summer months, and as you can see, these visiting school children loved coming along for the ride.

The trams are a great tourist attraction and well over 100 years old – the last still in service anywhere in the world. The horses are specially bred for the job and are well looked after when they retire. Sounds good to me!

"I get really fed up posing for these daft photographs." That's what Billy, the horse, was whispering in my ear!

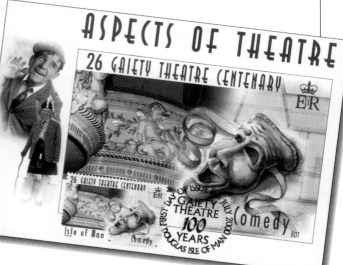

This is what first brought me to the Isle of Man all those years ago for a summer season – the **Gaiety Theatre**. Designed by the great **Frank Matcham**, it's been restored to its former splendour under the watchful eye of manager **Mervyn Stokes**, and he's done a fantastic job. And when Isle of Man Post produced a special issue Gaiety Theatre stamp, guess who got his face on it?

Fun and games aboard the **Isle of Man Steam Packet** ferry **Ben my Chree**. I've definitely got a mutiny on my hands! Captain **Roger Moore** (not 007) and Captain **Ken Crellin** are pulling no punches.

These high-visibility striped walls are features of the mountain road over **Snaefell** – designed to prevent motorists from going over the edge!

A view towards the north-east coastline, with **Ramsey** in the distance.

This is in my part of the world — the lighthouse at **Maughold Head**, which overlooks Ramsey.

Feeding time at **Garey Ford** near Ramsey.

I'D BE A FOOL TO LIVE ANYWHERE ELSE

A lovely view of **Ramsey**, showing the Queen's Pier and the twin breakwater, with the bay beyond.

100

It's no good – I just can't persuade **Dave Duke**, the Isle of Man's Police Community Officer of the Year, that he'd learn a lot from watching PC Norman Pitkin at work in my 1962 film **On the Beat**.

Wild and wondeful – the **Ayres**.

Point of Ayre lighthouse. If I take a few more steps to my left I'll be in Scotland!

The salesman said it goes like a rocket, so I'm thinking about trading in the BMW.

"It has been my pleasure to know Norman for many years both in his capacity as an entertainer and as a Charity Fund Raiser. It never ceases to amaze me the boundless energy Norman has for every project he takes on and the number of local charities he has helped over the years.
Norman is always a great Ambassador for the Isle of Man and none more so than during the Global Challenge Yacht Race when his help was invaluable. Norman continues to show us the lighter side of life."

Richard Corkill
Chief Minister of the Isle of Man

After these words of praise and thanks from **Richard Corkill**, Norman feels entitled to take his seat on the front bench with an important politician!